Dedicated to
Mary Threse

You inspire me and everyone around
you so much and I am blessed
to have you in my life.

Happy Birthday, Aunty Mary.

Love you lots!

Words of
ENCOURAGEMENT
(POV: Winter Magic)

Copyright © 2023 Janice J

All rights reserved.

Words of ENCOURAGEMENT
(POV: Winter Magic)

This season brings me back to childhood memories of school breaks and Christmas. Decorating the tree, listening to carols, the wondrous smell of cookies baking, and wrapping presents (and trying to guess them!) are always cherished moments that I keep close to my heart. Home Alone 2 will always and forever be my favorite holiday movie. Snow was something I only experienced through TV back then. I felt a sense of awe and wonder when I experienced snow for the first time. That magical feeling never left me.

I hope you are encouraged by the words inspired by this enchanting season.

Thank you, thank you, thank you.

JANICE J

As the first snow falls, it is filled with change, hope, and beauty. Transform into the version you want to be, hope for the best outcome, and enjoy the beauty of who you are.

Savor

the beauty of fresh snowfall on the ground. It coats the ground with a magical path just for you.

Close your

eyes, touch your heart and breathe in the crisp winter air. This is your moment of mindfulness.

Just like snowflakes, you are unique and wonderfully made. Learn to accept that there is only one you and you bring so much glow into this bleak world. You sparkle!

Your goodness warms the whole room like a comforting, cozy fireplace during a cold winter night. You are extraordinary and so special. Remember this.

Put on your

mittens and face the day! You can face anything that comes your way. Draw from your experiences and inner strength. You are always wiser and more resilient than you believe.

The winter winds

will blow away your doubts and fears. Inhale the cool air and feel your confidence build with every breath you take.

Let your worries melt like snow. Sometimes we may overthink a situation. That is perfectly normal. Take some time away from it and relook at it when our worries no longer overshadow the situation.

Envelop yourself with love, kindness, and happiness. You are a little spot of sunshine on a cold winter's day.

Surround

yourself with people who give you the warm feeling of sitting by a fireplace. It's comfortable enough for you to open your heart and share your dreams and inhibitions.

Make yourself a cup of hot cocoa and enjoy the moment. Use your five senses to enjoy your drink - sight, smell, touch, taste, and hearing. There's so much magic in a cup of hot cocoa!

Winter comes

with fun moments. Make snowmen and have friendly snowball fights! Always look for ways to make life fun and exciting. You hold the power to add more smiles and laughter to your life.

Glide through

challenges like skating on ice. Keep moving forward and pivot when needed. You will eventually find the answer you need.

The peace

of walking amongst the snow-covered trees and snowdrops blooming is a little joy that you can experience during this season. May you carry this peace throughout the day with you.

Send out a little love and kindness to those who need it most during this season. Some may be going through tough moments and are struggling. Your kindness will be a little flicker of comfort for them.

You shine

as bright as the northern lights. Keep radiating your authenticity and captivating the world with your beautiful heart.

Wake up and sleigh the day. You manage how your day goes. Choose to twinkle today!

You are

like the bright, brilliant ray of sunshine shining on a white winter day. Never dim your light for anything or anyone.

Build

your confidence and sculpt the future you want. You create what you desire.

Words are

powerful. It can warm or chill someone's day. You always have a choice to use your power to uplift and encourage others.

You are

a snow angel in my life! Wake up today and decide to do a random act of kindness to a stranger.

Find ways to

add fairy lights to a gloomy day. Listening to music that uplifts your spirits or even just telling someone how much you appreciate them can brighten up the day. There are always moments to be grateful for.

Giving comes

in many forms. Giving can be free...Give your best when you do something. Give a listening ear to someone who needs it. Give time for your loved ones.

Look up

at the clear winter skies at night and marvel at the beautiful stars. You shine just as brightly as they do. You add your own little twinkle in the vastness of the Universe.

Do things

that give you a happy feeling in your heart. Reading by the fireplace, going sledding, watching feel-good movies...Adding just a small thing that brings you joy can make your day better.

Explore the

beauty of nature - the frost on plants, snow-capped mountains, fresh snow, and majestic pine trees. We can learn so much from nature. Amidst the cold, they thrive, and their beauty comes through. It is the same with you. Your inner strength can withstand any cold and shine through.

Be grateful

that you get another day to breathe in the cool, frosty air. Cherish and make the best of it. Getting caught up in the past or worrying about the future is just going to affect the present moment. Take a breath and smile at this beautiful gift of life!

Some

relationships may not be able to withstand the harsh, cold moments. It is okay. Some relationships are only here for a season. Let go with grace and be grateful for the moments shared.

Find your favorite person and tell them how grateful you are to have them in your life! A little gesture goes a long way. It never hurts to share how warm they make you feel with their presence.

Go at your

own pace. Some ideas need more research and hibernating time before they can come to fruition. There are no set rules to achieve your dreams within a certain timeframe. Live by your own rules and navigate life the way that resonates best with you.

You may be going through an internal avalanche right now. Shine your beacon and seek for help. You do not have to go through it alone. There are helping hands out there if you're willing to ask.

Shovel

your doubts and insecurities
away. Pave the path that
leads to your happiness,
peace, and success.

You stand out

bright and vibrant just like a Christmas tree lighted up at night. No external force can fade your inner light. You are evergreen.

Winter is a

state of mind. It's your choice if you want it to be cold, dark, and harsh or if it is going to be a wonderland with lots of laughter and love. Make the best of every situation and condition you are faced with. It always begins at the mind. Make life magical!

People may
disappoint and shatter your
world. Remember who you
are and choose not to reflect
the same towards them. You
are better than that.

Be kind.

The world is cold enough. Let your kindness envelop the world in a warm hug, spreading love and hope.

Your smile

can melt the coldest heart. A simple gesture of a smile may light up someone's day. Share your smile with someone today.

Freeze

thoughts that no longer serve you. Fill your mind with possibilities, love, compassion, kindness, and joy. Take care of your mind, as it can easily be influenced.

Ground yourself

and stand tall like the snow-covered mountains. No matter what they endure, they continue to stand their ground. You can do the same. Build your strong foundation and stand tall!

Take a moment

to savor the treats and seasonal fruits of Winter. What fond memory does it evoke? Bring that feeling of beautiful nostalgia as you begin your day and create more memorable moments.

Believe in the

magic of miracles. When you believe, you can achieve what your heart desires. Be bold and start painting your desires as bright and beautiful as the Northern Lights.

Reach out

to your loved ones this season. Now is always the perfect time to do so. They may not be able to make it back during the holidays but do let them know that they are remembered and loved.

Set up

a cozy place just for you. This is your happy place, to just be and enjoy the present moment. We all deserve a little place of peace amid chaos.

Hold tight

during this sleigh ride called Life! We may go through snowstorms and avalanches, but we will also go through fun moments. Marvel at the beauty of spruce trees while sledding down a slope and landing in a cloud of snow!

Never lose

your sense of wonder. Look around, there is bound to be beauty and magic of the season around you.

There's something about Winter that makes us feel warm and tingly at the same time! A wonderful time to connect with yourself, your loved ones, and with nature. There's always a magical feeling in the air!

Embrace

both the naughty and nice parts of you. That's what makes you, YOU. Celebrate the unique soul that you are!

Warm up

to the idea that you can do anything you set your heart and mind to. The first step is to believe that it is possible. Then, watch the magic unfold!

Scrape away

the doubts and insecurities by asking yourself if there is any truth to it. If there is, look at it objectively and see how you can improve yourself. If there isn't, then set yourself free and let them go.

Showing mercy

and kindness to someone
who needs it the most is like a
warm hug that melts away
the chills on a snow day.

You are

a gem. Continue to shine and sparkle! You are a unique, special, and marvelous individual. Embrace all of you and keep being the treasure that you are.

Close your

eyes and enjoy the wonder of Winter. The smell of cookies baking, the crackle of fire, the warmth of a hug...Magical moments are made up of simple things that we take for granted.

Savor the sound of silence and the feeling of stillness that comes with snowfall. It is a wonderful time to learn from nature. Sometimes we must act, and sometimes we need to be still and wait. It is the balance of Life.

Directions to

make the perfect wreath: decorate it with pinecones, baubles, and holly. Sprinkle some good intentions, tie in some love and hope, and finally hang it up with joy and peace.

You are the

best gift that you can give the world. Unwrap your fears and go for your dreams. It doesn't matter how big or small your dream is. What matters is that you believe in yourself and take that leap of faith to achieve it.

You are a beacon of light on a dark Winter's night. Keep shining your truth out there and guiding others. I'm here for it!

Your inner beauty shines through like Christmas lights. It brings a smile to those who see you. You twinkle and shine!

Cloak yourself

with forgiveness, compassion, and a loving heart this holiday season. The world needs more of this right now.

Sing and dance to your favorite tunes of this Season. There is something so nostalgic about listening to familiar tunes while baking and decorating for the holidays.

Sometimes

all you need is a listening ear and a warm hug to make your day better. When all else fails, get the eggnog!

Being present

is sometimes the best gift
that you can give someone.
Holding space for them to
truly be who they are without
judgment is the loveliest thing
that can unfold in this
situation.

Steer away from mulling on the past. It will only take away the beauty of the present moment. The current moment deserves your full attention.

Set the

night up with warm blankets and watch a holiday movie. We all need moments to relax and unwind.

This is

a wonderful time to build core memories with your loved ones. Make this season a memorable one. What's your most treasured winter memory?

Trace a

heart on a frosted window to brighten someone's day. There are many little ways to make life beautiful. ❤️

If you're

getting cold feet from decisions you made to improve your life, that is okay. You won't fully know how a decision will unfold until you take it. You gain from each decision made as it will teach you valuable lessons in this school of Life. I'm proud of you.

Happiness

is getting a gift for your beloved and knowing that they are going to love it. This is a wonderful season to show your love through giving.

All is calm within you. Trust your instincts and do your best.

Sunsets

are magical, but moonrise is even more spectacular. Gaze upon the wintry night and watch the Cold Moon rise. You are just like the moon, rising brightly amidst the darkness.

Friendships

transcends time and distance. Cherish your friends, near and far. Be grateful for friends who stay with you during the good and frosty moments in life.

Take a moment

and hug yourself. The year is ending, and you've gone through many hurdles and celebrations. Appreciate every moment. Be proud of everything you've overcome and smile knowing that you are still standing.

You are truly enough.

Words of Encouragement
(POV: Winter Magic)

Made in the USA
Las Vegas, NV
03 December 2023